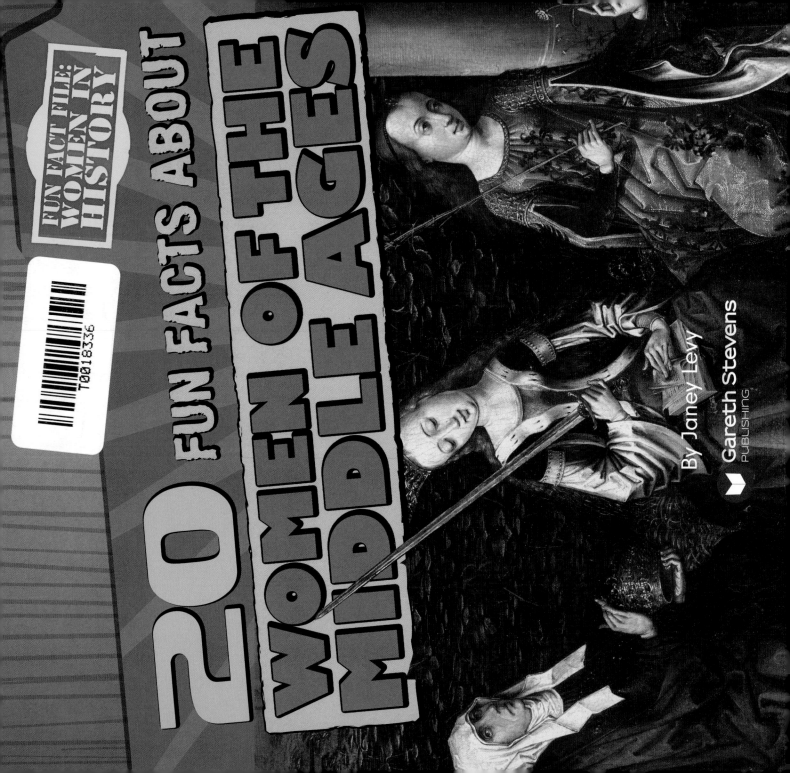

FUN FACT FILE: WOMEN IN HISTORY

20 FUN FACTS ABOUT

WOMEN OF THE MIDDLE AGES

By Janey Levy

Gareth Stevens
PUBLISHING

Please visit our website, www.garethstevens.com. For a free color catalog of all our high-quality books, call toll free 1-800-542-2595 or fax 1-877-542-2596.

Library of Congress Cataloging-in-Publication Data

Levy, Janey.
20 fun facts about women of the Middle Ages / Janey Levy.
    pages cm. — (Fun fact file: women in history)
Includes bibliographical references and index.
ISBN 978-1-4824-2824-7 (pbk.)
ISBN 978-1-4824-2825-4 (6 pack)
ISBN 978-1-4824-2826-1 (library binding)
1. Women–History–Middle Ages, 500–1500–Juvenile literature. 2. Middle Ages–Juvenile literature. 3.
Civilization, Medieval–Juvenile literature. I. Title. II. Title: Twenty fun facts about women of the Middle Ages.
HQ1143.L49 2016
305.4009'02–dc23

2014049861

First Edition

Published in 2016 by
Gareth Stevens Publishing
111 East 14th Street, Suite 349
New York, NY 10003

Copyright © 2016 Gareth Stevens Publishing

Designer: Samantha DeMartin
Editor: Kristen Rajczak

Photo credits: Cover, p. 1 Print Collector/Hulton Fine Art Collection/Getty Images; pp. 5, 7 DEA Picture Library/De Agostini/Getty Images; pp. 6, 13 (nobles) DEA/A. De Gregorio/De Agostini/Getty Images; p. 8 De Agostini Picture Library/De Agostini Picture Library/Getty Images; pp. 9, 16, Leemage/Universal Images Group/Getty Images; p. 10 Limbourg brothers/Wikimedia Commons; pp. 11, 13 (peasants) DEA/A. De Gregorio/De Agostini Picture Library/Getty Images; p. 12 LTL/Universal Images Group/Getty Images; pp. 13 (king), 17, 21, 25, 29 Hulton Archive/Hulton Archive/Getty Images; pp. 13 (merchants), 14 DEA/J. E. Bulloz/De Agostini/Getty Images; p. 13 (knight), 23 Heritage Images/Hulton Fine Art Collection/Getty Images; p. 15 DEA/M. Seemuller/De Agostini/Getty Images; p. 18 Master of James IV of Scotland/Wikimedia Commons; p. 19 Giuseppe Rivelli/Wikimedia Commons; p. 20 Culture Club/Hulton Archive/Getty Images; p. 22 Leemage/Universal Images Group Editorial/Getty Images; p. 26 Apic/Hulton Archive/Getty Images; p. 27 Miscellanea medica XVIII/Wikimedia Commons.

All rights reserved. No part of this book may be reproduced in any form without permission in writing from the publisher, except by a reviewer.

Printed in the United States of America

CPSIA compliance information: Batch #CS15GS. For further information contact Gareth Stevens, New York, New York at 1-800-542-2595.

Contents

Words in the glossary appear in **bold** type the first time they are used in the text.

The Middle Ages was the time between the classical world of ancient Greece and Rome and the rebirth of classical ideals during the Renaissance. It lasted over 1,000 years, from before 500 to about 1500.

Great artworks, buildings, music, and books were created during this period. But life was hard—especially for women. Men ruled society. Women were considered lesser creatures and had few rights and little freedom. And yet—well, keep reading. You'll see. These women will surprise you!

During the Middle Ages, or medieval period, most people lived in the countryside or in small villages. But busy, crowded towns and cities also existed.

FACT 1

The top jobs for women were wife and mother. Most women married while they were teenagers.

Women commonly had no say about whom they married. Marriages were arranged either by their parents or by other adults with power over them. For wealthy young women, their marriage was often arranged for the **political** benefit of their parents.

This picture shows the wedding of a wealthy couple. Records show that women could pay a fine to be allowed to choose their own husband or to stay single.

FACT 2

The law recognized no identity for a married woman separate from that of her husband.

A husband made decisions that stood for his wife as well as himself. A woman was supposed to be her husband's "helpmeet" and help him with his work, whatever it was.

Here, a man gathers grapes while a woman—perhaps his wife—lifts a bucket of grapes to dump them into a large tub. In the tub, a young man—perhaps their son—presses the grapes with his feet, the first step in making wine.

FACT 3

A wife's work was often deadly.

Wives were in charge of the work needed to run the home. Many women drowned in public wells and ponds while getting water for their home.

Washing clothes was also dangerous. The large tubs of boiling water could tip over and burn women.

A wife's work was hard even when it wasn't deadly. Most wives made clothes for their family, but before they could do that, they had to spin thread and **weave** cloth.

FACT 4

Having a baby could be deadly.

Some believe as many

as one out of every five

women died giving birth.

Problems that can be

easily treated today

were often deadly

in the Middle Ages.

They could be deadly

for the baby as well.

Women called midwives took
care of mothers during the birth
of their baby.

Peasant Women
at the Bottom

FACT 5

Peasants were at the bottom of society and had the hardest lives. Peasant women were a step below peasant men.

Records from medieval England show women working in farm fields were paid about two-thirds what men were paid for the same work. Cutting crops and making hay were hard, sometimes backbreaking labor.

Tasks such as cutting grain required workers to spend much of their time bent over in a position that was hard on their back.

Long hours working in the fields with heavy tools such as these built up strong muscles, and the muscles in turn built up big bones to support them.

FACT 6

Peasant women's hard life gave them big bones.

Skeletons found at a small medieval English village show peasant women had bigger **muscles** and bones than women who lived in cities. That came from doing hard farmwork in addition to caring for children, cooking, gardening, making and mending clothes, and doing other jobs around the home.

FACT 7

In addition to everything else she did, a peasant wife might earn money by running a small business.

Peasant women sometimes earned money by selling eggs or vegetables from their personal garden. They might also make more ale or cloth than their family needed and sell the extra.

Medieval Society

Medieval society was arranged like a pyramid. Most people were peasants, and they were at the bottom. Just above them were merchants and craftspeople, who lived in towns and cities. At the next level were the knights, who kept people safe and fought in wars. Above the knights were the nobles. The king was at the top.

king

nobles

knights

merchants and craftspeople

peasants

FACT 8

Although towns and cities offered many different kinds of work, it was still a man's world.

Towns and cities had craftspeople who made all types of goods and merchants who sold them. But they had to belong to groups called **guilds**, and many guilds wouldn't allow women. So women mostly worked for their father or husband.

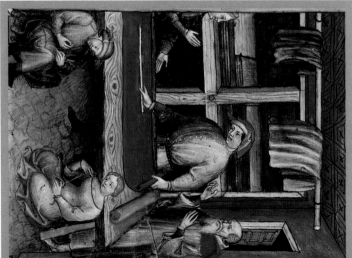

FACT 9

Even in a world ruled by men, women were welcomed in some guilds.

Guilds for trades connected to tasks women commonly did in the home were often filled with women. These included guilds for weavers, cloth dyers, ale makers, and picklers.

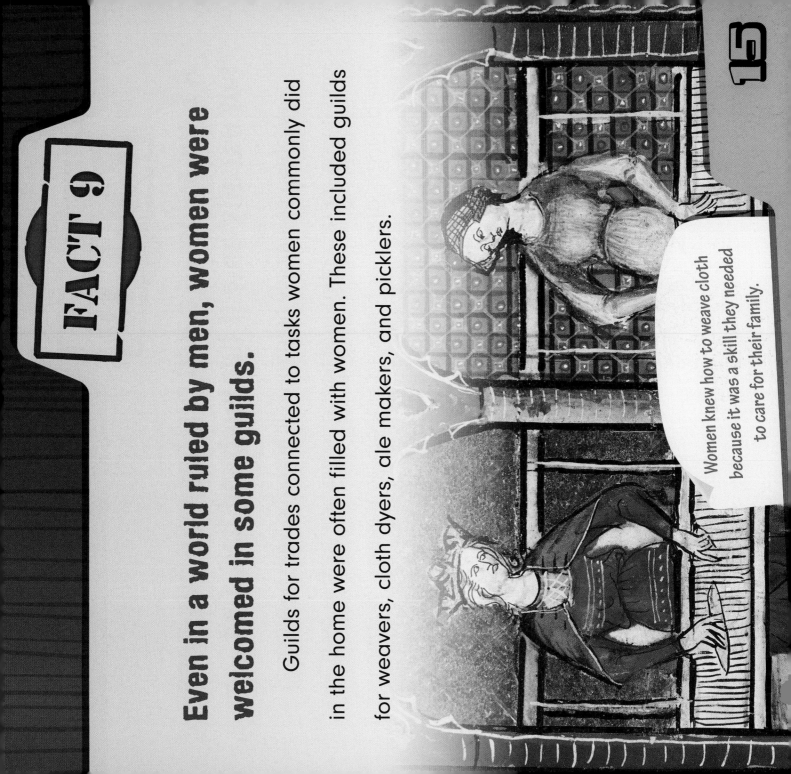

Women knew how to weave cloth because it was a skill they needed to care for their family.

FACT 10

A townswoman could run her own business, but usually only if her husband had died.

Women commonly helped their husband with his work, and it was an accepted practice for a woman to take over the business after her husband's death. In this way, women became **butchers**, shoemakers, builders, and many other kinds of craftspeople.

Bread bought from a baker was likely to have been baked by a woman—but no one would say so.

FACT 11

Noble and royal women had time to party.

Noble and royal women had servants to help them care

for their children and

do housework. That

left them time to take

part in activities just

for pleasure, such

as dancing, playing

games, and hunting.

Like medieval noblemen, noblewomen hunted for fun.

17

FACT 12

Even parties could be work.

Noble and royal women were expected to attend social events at the castles of other nobles and the king, whether they wanted to or not. These events included dances and great feasts where they might eat food covered with real gold!

Foods served at a medieval feast might include lamprey, eel, peacock, swan, partridge, and small songbirds.

FACT 13

When a nobleman wasn't home, his wife took over his duties — and his power.

When a nobleman

was away at war or at the

king's court, his wife was

in charge. She oversaw all

business on their property

and acted as judge in the

local law court. If she had

to, she would even

fight off anyone who

attacked their land!

Matilda of Tuscany was a noblewoman who was famous for her military accomplishments. She actually put on armor and led soldiers into battle!

FACT 14

Joanna of Flanders, who was married to the duke of Brittany, took up arms and put on armor to fight for her land.

After Joanna's husband died, others tried to take over her land. To keep her territory safe, she led an attack on the enemy's camp. She set fire to the camp and destroyed it. For that, she became known as Fiery Joanna.

Joanna advised the women of her town to take charge of their own safety.

FACT 15

Joan of Arc, the most famous medieval woman warrior, was born a peasant.

Joan was born in France around 1412, when France and England were at war.

When she was about 17, she talked the French king into letting her lead an army against the English. She won many battles.

After losing some battles, Joan was captured by the enemy. She was tried for crimes, sentenced, and then tied to a stake and burned to death.

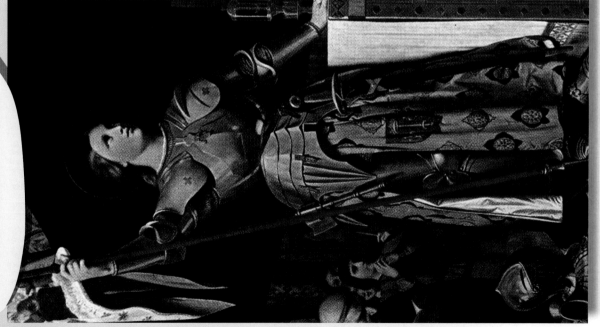

FACT 16

A townswoman named Jeanne Laisne gained fame fighting with an ax.

In 1472, the duke of Burgundy attacked the French town of Beauvais. The townspeople—including the women—fought back. Jeanne fought off the man carrying the Burgundian flag with a small ax. This gave the townspeople the bravery needed to win the battle.

Jeanne became known as Jeanne Hachette after the battle. "Hachette" is the French word for "hatchet," which is another name for a small ax.

FACT 17

A military order of knighthood just for women existed in Spain.

Most orders were for men, but one called the Order of the Hatchet was founded in 1149 in a part of Spain called Catalonia. It was to honor women who fought to guard the town of Tortosa.

An order was a group of knights bound by a set of rules that governed their conduct.

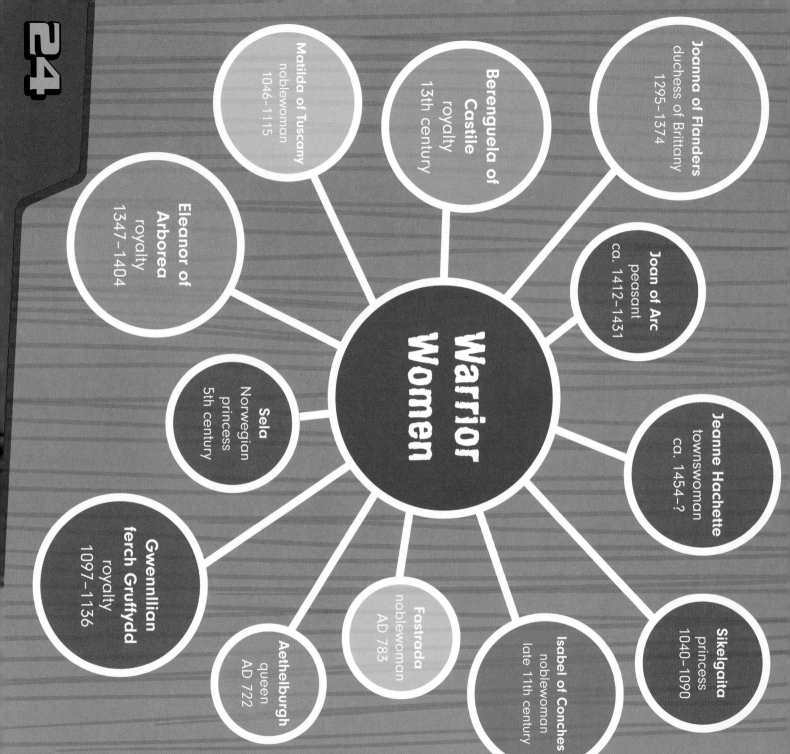

Warrior Women

Joanna of Flanders
duchess of Brittany
1295-1374

Matilda of Tuscany
noblewoman
1046-1115

Berenguela of Castile
royalty
13th century

Eleanor of Arborea
royalty
1347-1404

Joan of Arc
peasant
ca. 1412-1431

Sela
Norwegian princess
5th century

Jeanne Hachette
townswoman
ca. 1454-?

Gwennllian ferch Gruffydd
royalty
1097-1136

Aethelburgh
queen
AD 722

Fastrada
noblewoman
AD 783

Isabel of Conches
noblewoman
late 11th century

Sikelgaita
princess
1040-1090

FACT 18

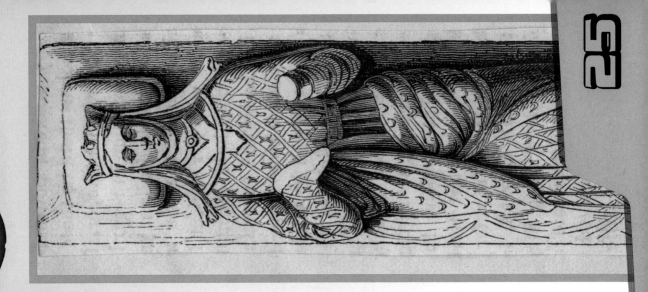

Eleanor of Aquitaine, the queen of England, tried to overthrow her husband.

Eleanor, a French noblewoman, married Henry II of England in 1152. He became king in 1154. Their sons **revolted** against Henry in 1173, and Eleanor—angry at Henry—supported her sons. The revolt failed, and Henry locked Eleanor up.

Eleanor remained in prison until Henry II died in 1189.

FACT 19

Christine de Pisan was a famous and successful writer at a time when few women were educated.

Christine grew up at the court of the French king, where her father worked. She married at 15. When her husband died 10 years later, she took up writing to support her three young children. She's especially famous for her books honoring women and their accomplishments.

Christine is shown here bowing before a queen and presenting one of her books to the queen. Some of the most powerful people of the time ordered books from Christine.

FACT 20

Trotula was a woman doctor whose books on women's medicine were still being used five centuries later.

Trotula lived in Italy in the 11th century. She was a famous teacher at one of the first **universities** in Europe, which was located at Salerno. Her books covered subjects ranging from childbirth to skin problems to makeup.

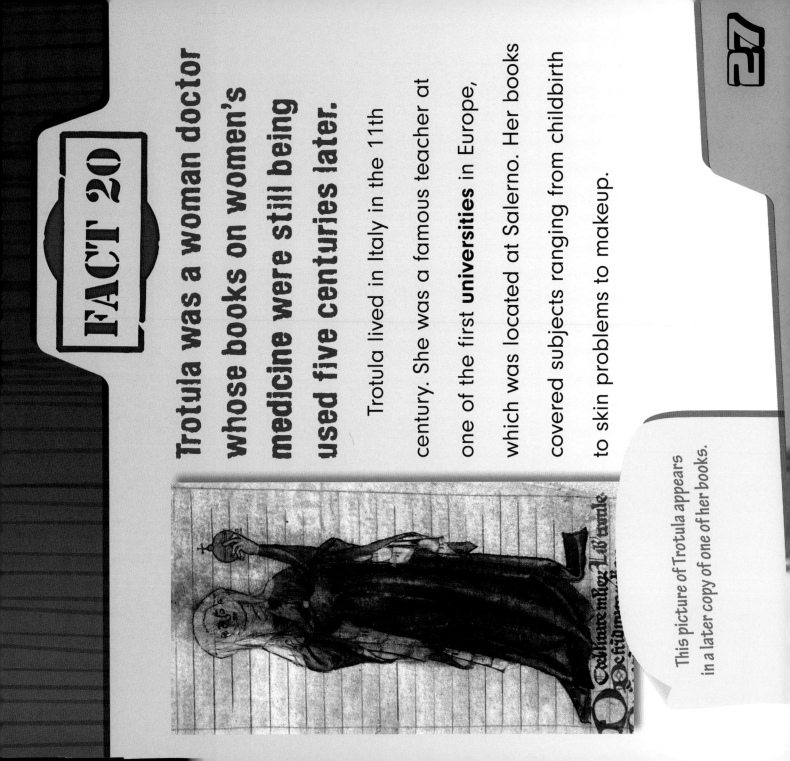

This picture of Trotula appears in a later copy of one of her books.

Wonderful Medieval Women

From peasants to queens, medieval women had hard lives, without the comforts and modern tools we take for granted. Even everyday tasks were filled with danger and could be deadly. Yet these women pushed on, even though society didn't honor their work. They did everything expected of them, which often meant they did more than men.

Some women broke the rules and went beyond the limits society placed on them. They became warriors, writers, and doctors. Medieval women were truly wonderful!

Forget about the kind of weak medieval princess you might read about in a storybook. These women were strong!

Glossary

butcher: someone who prepares and sells animal meat

guild: a society of merchants or members of a craft established to advance the interests of the craft and the guild's members

identity: individual existence

medicine: the science and art dealing with keeping health and avoiding sickness

muscle: one of the parts of the body that allow movement

peasant: a person at the bottom of medieval society who worked the land

political: having to do with matters of government and power

revolt: to turn against an established authority. Also, an uprising against an established authority.

skeleton: the boney frame of the body

university: a school for higher learning

warrior: a soldier

weave: to make cloth by passing threads back and forth over and under each other

For More Information

Books

Allen, Kathy. *The Horrible, Miserable Middle Ages: The Disgusting Details About Life During Medieval Times*. Mankato, MN: Capstone Press, 2010.

Groves, Marsha. *Manners and Customs in the Middle Ages*. New York, NY: Crabtree Publishing, 2006.

Langley, Andrew. *Medieval Life*. New York, NY: DK Publishing, 2011.

Websites

Medieval Women
www.medieval-life-and-times.info/medieval-women/
Read biographies of famous women of the Middle Ages, and find out more about life during this time.

Medieval Women
www.ancientfortresses.org/medieval-women.htm
Learn about life during the Middle Ages and what it was like to be a woman then.

Publisher's note to educators and parents: Our editors have carefully reviewed these websites to ensure that they are suitable for students. Many websites change frequently, however, and we cannot guarantee that a site's future contents will continue to meet our high standards of quality and educational value. Be advised that students should be closely supervised whenever they access the Internet.

Index